Dr. Frenchy's
Bible ABCs
A Colorful, Multilingual Alphabet Book

Dr. Karen Lea French
Doctor Frenchy

Illustrated by Cynthia Alford

 PUBLICATION
CONSULTANTS
We Believe In The Power Of Authors
PO Box 221974 Anchorage, Alaska 99522-1974
www.publicationconsultants.com

ISBN 1-59433-016-6

Library of Congress Catalog Card Number: 2004095360

Copyright 2004 by Dr. Karen Lea French
—First Printing 2004—
—Second Printing 2009—
—Third Printing 2019—

Manufactured in Canada.

Dedication

Dedicated to my parents:
Richard T. and Natalie Kraft French,
for their love, encouragement,
and their faith in me.

Also dedicated to
teachers of God's word.

Angels
- Anjos
- Anjos
- Ángeles
- Zanj yo
- Ангелы
- Les anges
- Mga anghel
- Ангели

Bible
- Bíblia
- Biblia
- Biblia
- Bibla
- Библия
- La Bible
- Biblia
- Біблія

Cross
- Cruz
- Cruz
- Cruz
- Lakwa
- Крест
- La croix
- Krus
- Хрест

Disciples
- Discípulos
- Disciplos
- Discípulos
- Disip yo
- Последователи
- Les disciples
- Mga disipulo
- Послідовники

Easter
- Páscoa
- Pascoa
- Pascua
- Pak
- Пасха
- Pâques
- Mahal na Araw
- Великдень

Faith
- Fé
- Fe
- Fe
- Lafwa
- Вера
- La foi
- Pananalig
- Віра

Giver
- Doador
- Doar
- Donante
- Ap bay
- Даритель
- Le donateur
- Nagbibigay
- Даритель

Heaven
- Céu
- Ceu
- Paraíso
- Syel
- Небеса
- Le paradis
- Langit
- Небеса

Inn
- Hospedaria
- Hospedaria
- Posada
- Lotel
- Гостиница
- L'auberge
- Bahay-panuluyan
- Готель

Jesus
- Jesus
- Jesus
- Jesús
- Jezi
- Иисус
- Jésus
- Hesus
- Іісус

Kind
- Gentil
- Carinhosa
- Amable
- Espes
- Доброта
- Gentils
- Mabait
- Доброта

Love
- Amar
- Amor
- Amor
- Renmen
- Любить
- L'amour
- Pag-ibig
- Любити

Missionary
- Missionário
- Missionario
- Missionero
- Misyone
- Миссионер
- Le missionnaire
- Misyonaryo
- Міссі онер

Noah's Ark
- Arca de Noé
- Arca de Noe
- Arca de Nóe
- Bato Noah
- Ноин Ковчег
- L'arche de Noé
- Arka ni Noah
- Ноін Човен

Obey
- Obedecer
- Obedecer
- Obedecer
- Obeyi
- Повиноваться
- Obéir
- Sumunod
- Повинуватися

Pray
- Orar
- Orar
- Rezar
- Priye
- Молиться
- Prier
- Magdasal
- Молитися

Quiet
- Quieto
- Silencio
- Silencio
- Silans
- Быь Послушным
- La tranquillité
- Tumahimik
- БулиСлухняним

Rejoice
- Alegrar-se
- Regozijar-se
- Alegrarse
- Rejwi
- Радоваться
- Se réjouir
- Magsaya
- Радіти

Salvation
- Salvação
- Salvacao
- Salvación
- Delivre
- Спасение
- Le salut
- Kaligtasan
- Спасіння

Testimony
- Testemunho
- Testemunho
- Testimonio
- Temwayaj
- Свидетельство
- Le témoignage
- Katunayan
- Свідчення

Understands
- Entender
- Entender
- Entender
- Komprann
- Понимает
- Il comprend
- Naiintindihan
- Розумі`

Verses
- Versículos
- Versos
- Versos
- Vese yo
- Стихи
- Les vers
- Berso
- Вірші

Worship
- Adoração
- Adorar
- Adorar
- Adore
- Поклоняться
- La pratique religieuse
- Sambahin
- Поклонитися

Explains
- Explicar
- Explicar
- Explicar
- Esplike
- Объясняет
- Explique
- Ipaliwanag
- Поясню`

Young
- Jovens
- Jovens
- Jóvenes
- Jenn
- Молодые
- Jeune
- Mga bata
- Молоді

Zeal
- Zelo
- Monte siao
- Fervor
- Zes
- Рвение
- Le zèle
- Sigasig
- Стремління

These are the colors for the different languages when you see the words on the page:

- English
- Brazilian Portuguese
- Portuguese
- Spanish
- Creole
- Russian
- French
- Filipino/Tagalog
- Ukrainian

Angels

Anjos

Anjos

Ángeles

Zanj yo

Ангелы

Les anges

Mga anghel

Ангели

Angels are everywhere
and always protect us.

Bible

Bíblia
Biblia
Biblia
Bibla
Библия
La Bible
Biblia
Біблія

The **Bible** is the word of God.

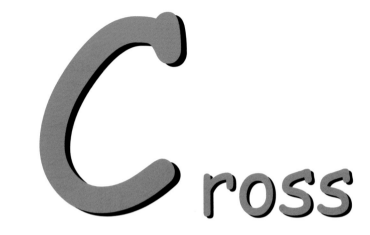

Cross

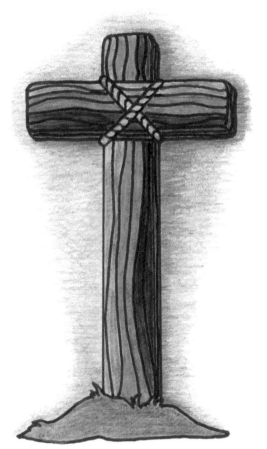

Cruz

Cruz

Cruz

Lakwa

Крест

La croix

Krus

Хрест

Jesus died on the **cross** to save us from our sins.

Disciples

Discípulos

Disciplos

Discípulos

Disip yo

Последователи

Les disciples

Mga disipulo

Послідовники

Jesus had 12 disciples.

Easter

Páscoa

Pascoa

Pascua

Pak

Пасха

Pâques

Mahal na Araw

Великдень

Easter is the celebration of Jesus being resurrected.

Faith

Fé

Fe

Fe

Lafwa

Bepa

La foi

Pananalig

Bipa

Faith is believing in what we cannot see.

Giver

Doador

Doar

Donante

Ap bay

Даритель

Le donateur

Nagbibigay

Даритель

God loves a cheerful **giver**.

Heaven

Céu

Ceu

Paráiso

Syel

Небеса

Le paradis

Langit

Небеса

God lives in Heaven.

I nn

Hospedaria

Hospedaria

Posada

Lotel

Гостиница

L'auberge

Bahay-panuluyan

Готель

Jesus was born in a manger because there was no room at the inn.

Jesus

Jesus

Jesus

Jesús

Jezi

Иисус

Jésus

Hesus

Іісус

Jesus is the Son of God.

Kind

Gentil

Carinhosa

Amable

Espes

Доброта

Gentils

Mabait

Доброта

Jesus teaches us to be kind to one another.

Love

Amar

Amor

Amor

Renmen

Любить

L'amour

Pag-ibig

Любити

God wants us to
love one another.

Missionary

Missionário

Missionario

Missionero

Misyone

Миссионер

Le missionnaire

Misyonaryo

Місci онер

A **missionary** travels
to share the word of God.

Noah's Ark

Arca de Noé

Arca de Noe

Arca de Nóe

Bato Noah

Ноин Ковчег

L'arche de Noé

Arka ni Noah

Ноін Човен

God asked Noah to build an ark — **Noah's Ark**.

Obey

Obedecer
Obedecer
Obedecer
Obeyi
Повиноваться
Obéir
Sumunod
Повинуватися

Children should obey their parents.

Pray

Orar

Orar

Rezar

Priye

Молиться

Prier

Magdasal

Молитися

Pray to God every day.

Quiet

Quieto

Silencio

Silencio

Silans

Быть Послушным

La tranquillité

Tumahimik

Бути Слухняним

Be quiet and still to listen to God.

Rejoice

Alegrar-se

Regozijar-se

Alegrarse

Rejwi

Радоваться

Se réjouir

Magsaya

Радіти

Rejoice for the blessings we have.

Salvation

Salvação

Salvacao

Salvación

Delivre

Спасение

Le salut

Kaligtasan

Спасіння

We receive **salvation** through believing in Jesus and asking him to come into our hearts.

Testimony

Testemunho
Testemunho
Testimonio
Temwayaj
Свидетельство
Le témoignage
Katunayan
Свідчення

We share our belief in God through our testimony.

Understands

Entender

Entender

Entender

Komprann

Понимает

Il comprend

Naiintindihan

Розумі `

Jesus always **understands** when we are hurting.

Verses

Versículos

Versos

Versos

Vese yo

Стихи

Les vers

Berso

Вірші

I can learn and memorize **verses** from the Bible.

Worship

Adoração

Adorar

Adorar

Adore

Поклоняться

La pratique religieuse

Sambahin

Поклонитися

We go to church to worship God.

e✗plains

Explicar

Explicar

Explicar

Esplike

Объясняет

Explique

Ipaliwanag

Поясню`

The minister **explains** God's word through sermons and stories.

Young

Jovens

Jovens

Jóvenes

Jenn

Молодые

Jeune

Mga bata

Молоді

Young children are precious to Jesus.

#

Zelo

Monte siao

Fervor

Zes

Рвение

Le zèle

Sigasig

Стремління

Teach with **zeal!**

Further Learning

Test Your Bible Knowledge.

- How many Bible verses do you know?

- Find a partner (friend, parent, or teacher …) to share your Bible verses with.

- What other Bible words can you think of for each letter?

- Write your own Bible ABC book.

- What is your favorite Bible story?

- Tell someone, or write about, your favorite Bible story.

- How many languages do you know?

- Say the Bible ABC words in the different languages.

Cynthia Alford is a pastor's wife and homemaker who enjoys doing interior decorating and freelance art work. She received her degree in Commercial Art from the University of South Alabama.

Cynthia served as a preschool Sunday School worker for more than 23 years, beginning her service in that area when she was a teenager. She would regularly use her skill as an artist to create drawings and special projects for young children.

She and her husband Ken are the parents of two teenagers, Elizabeth and Andrew.

To contact Dr. French, or to order additional copies, write, e-mail, or call:
Dr. Karen Lea French
#508 1120 E. Huffman Road Ste. 23
Anchorage, Alaska 99515
907-229-2648
Email: DrFrenchy21@msn.com
Website: http://www.DrFrenchy.com

Additional Copies
1-5 books - $9.95
5 - 20 - $8 each
21 or more - $7 each

Organizations: Contact Dr. French for quantity discounts.